FISHING
RECORD BOOK

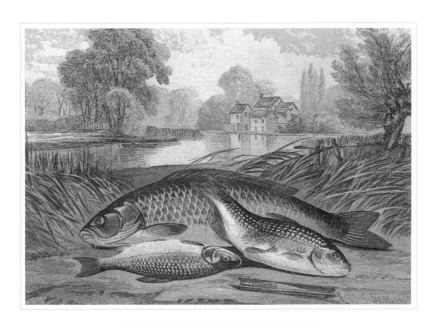

EBURY PRESS STATIONERY

Published in 1993 by Ebury Press Stationery
An imprint of Random House UK Ltd
Random House, 20 Vauxhall Bridge Road
London SW1V 2SA

Copyright © Random House UK Ltd 1993

Illustrations by permission of Nicholas Marchant-Lane

ISBN 0 09 177852 2

Set in Times
by FMT Colour Ltd, London SE1
Printed in Hongkong

Picture research by
Book Packaging and Marketing
Silverstone, Northants
Photography by
Viccari Photography, Bolney, Sussex

Front cover illustration
A. Rowland Knight, *Salmon, The First Leap.*
From a Tucks postcard, the *Oilette* series, circa 1905.

Back cover illustration
A. Rowland Knight, *A Hungry Pike*, oil on canvas, circa 1905

Title page illustration
H. L. Rolfe, *Carp and Roach*, coloured lithograph, 1870

PERSONAL DETAILS

NAME Graham McHardy

ADDRESS Moriah , Assynt St , Evanton ,
Ross-Shire , Scotland .   POST/ZIP CODE   IV16 9YG

TELEPHONE (HOME) 830810 (0349) (WORK)   FAX

ROD LICENCE DETAILS

RIVER LICENCE DETAILS   Evanton Angling Club 1993, 1994
Alness Angling Club 1995

RODS

	ROD	TYPE	LENGTH	REEL	A.F.T.M.	LINE	LEADER
1	Fly	IM6 Lurejlash	9½t	LC-80 Rimfly	6-8	Yellow Float	10ft (MAXIMA) 5-10 BS.
2	Fly	Airflow classic	10ft	Airflow alu.	7-8	Airflow float	6lb BS
3							
4							
5							
6							

Date	River	Fly/Bait	Weather
17th Aug '96	Rothiemurchus Trout Farm	Damzel	Warm Overcast
"	"	Montana	"
,,	"	Damzel	"
"	"	"	"
"	"	"	"
"	"	"	"
14th May 2000	Stonefield trout fisheries	Yellow & Green Fritz	Very hot / bright day
Sep '96	Tarvie lochs	Damzel	bright, slightly overcast
May '99	"	Viva hot head	Warm / overcast and humid

Water Conditions	Size	Species	Comments
Reasonable Still	2 lb	Rainbow Trout	Weren't Fighters
"	"	"	"
"	1½ lb	"	"
"	1½ lb	"	"
"	1 lb	"	"
"	1 lb	"	"
Reasonable still	10lb 6½oz 1lb 15oz	Rainbow trout	Put up a good fight, Several attempts to land the 10lb fish. Both lovely fish from top to bottom.
Rippled	2lb / 2½lb	"	Fine fishes all round
Rippled	1lb	"	A reasonable fish, not a fighter

DATE	RIVER	FLY/BAIT	WEATHER
1st Aug 1999	Stonefield lochs	Orange fritz	Very hot/sunny day

Water Conditions	Size	Species	Comments
Rippled	1 lb	Rainbow trout	Resonable fish. Fish only just hooked.

A. Rowland Knight, *Trout, Hooked but not landed.*
From a Tucks postcard, the *Oilette* series, circa 1905.

DATE	RIVER	FLY/BAIT	WEATHER

WATER CONDITIONS	SIZE	SPECIES	COMMENTS

Date	River	Fly/Bait	Weather

Water Conditions	Size	Species	Comments

Vintage fishing tackle, circa 1830-1900,
from the Marchant Lane Collection.

Date	River	Fly/Bait	Weather

Water Conditions	Size	Species	Comments

Date	River	Fly/Bait	Weather

Water Conditions	Size	Species	Comments

Date	River	Fly/Bait	Weather

Water Conditions	Size	Species	Comments

A. Rowland Knight, *A Hungry Pike*, oil on canvas, circa 1905.

Date	River	Fly/Bait	Weather

Water Conditions	Size	Species	Comments

Date	River	Fly/Bait	Weather

Water Conditions	Size	Species	Comments

Date	River	Fly/Bait	Weather

Water Conditions	Size	Species	Comments

NOTES

Mixed Still Life Fish including Trout, Tench,
Perch and Minnow, circa 1830, unsigned.

DATE	RIVER	FLY/BAIT	WEATHER

Water Conditions	Size	Species	Comments

DATE	RIVER	FLY/BAIT	WEATHER

Water Conditions	Size	Species	Comments

Date	River	Fly/Bait	Weather

Water Conditions	Size	Species	Comments

A selection of salmon flies mostly *Gut Eyed*, circa 1920.

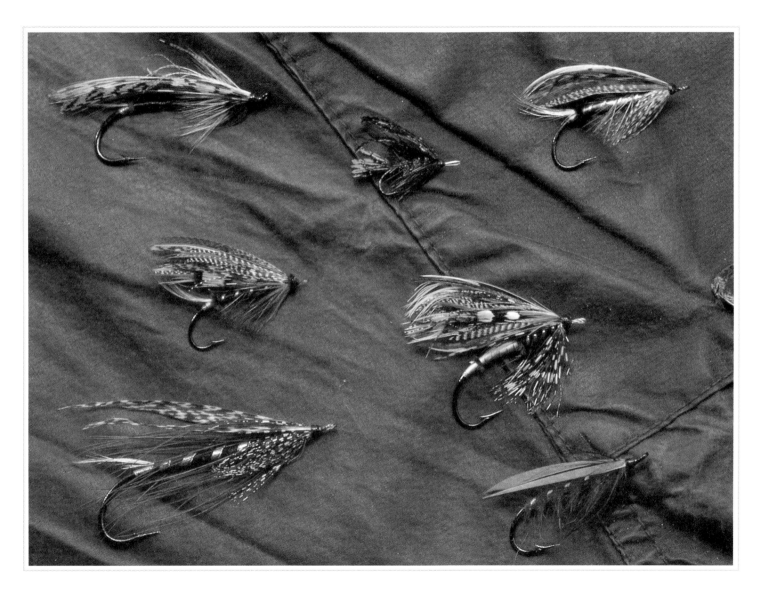

DATE	RIVER	FLY/BAIT	WEATHER

Water Conditions	Size	Species	Comments

Date	River	Fly/Bait	Weather

Water Conditions	Size	Species	Comments

Date	River	Fly/Bait	Weather

WATER CONDITIONS	SIZE	SPECIES	COMMENTS

A. Rowland Knight, *Salmon, The First Leap.*
From a Tucks postcard, the *Oilette* series, circa 1905.

Date	River	Fly/Bait	Weather

Water Conditions	Size	Species	Comments

Date	River	Fly/Bait	Weather

WATER CONDITIONS	SIZE	SPECIES	COMMENTS

Date	River	Fly/Bait	Weather

Water Conditions	Size	Species	Comments

R. Cleminson, *Roach, Still Life*, circa 1872.

Date	River	Fly/Bait	Weather

Water Conditions	Size	Species	Comments

Date	River	Fly/Bait	Weather

Water Conditions	Size	Species	Comments

Date	River	Fly/Bait	Weather

WATER CONDITIONS	SIZE	SPECIES	COMMENTS

H. L. Rolfe, *Hooked*, oil on canvas, circa 1867.
The painting was sent to a friend by H. L. Rolfe as
a gift for a day's fishing on the river Ver.

DATE	RIVER	FLY/BAIT	WEATHER

Water Conditions	Size	Species	Comments

Date	River	Fly/Bait	Weather

Water Conditions	Size	Species	Comments

A collection of mixed fishing tackle, circa 1850, including
a rare billhead captioned *I Bazin, 3 Duncan Place, Hackney*.

Date	River	Fly/Bait	Weather

Water Conditions	Size	Species	Comments

Date	River	Fly/Bait	Weather

WATER CONDITIONS	SIZE	SPECIES	COMMENTS

NOTES

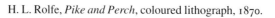

H. L. Rolfe, *Pike and Perch*, coloured lithograph, 1870.

DATE	RIVER	FLY/BAIT	WEATHER

Water Conditions	Size	Species	Comments

Date	River	Fly/Bait	Weather

Water Conditions	Size	Species	Comments

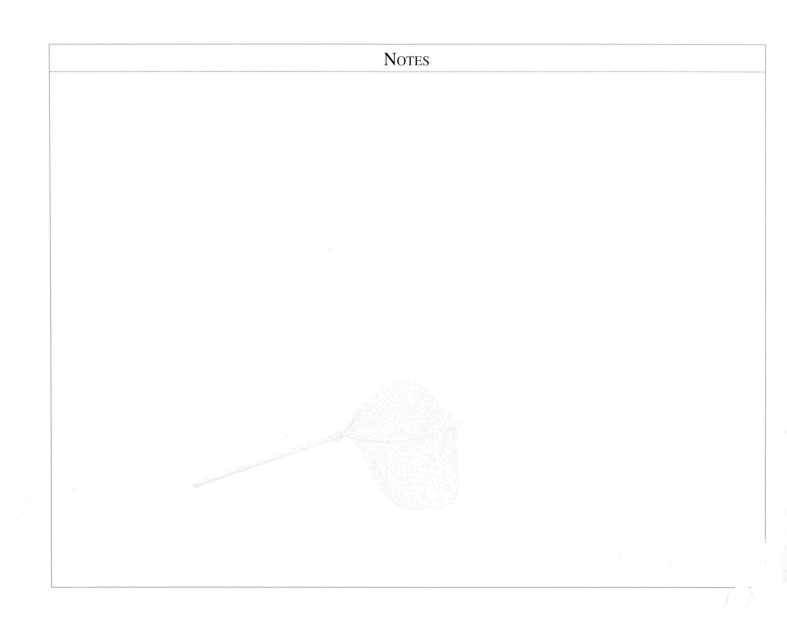